Composite Nation

Frontispiece from Frederick Douglass' *Narrative of the Life of Frederick Douglass, an American Slave*, 1845. Patricia D. Klingenstein Library, New-York Historical Society.

Composite Nation

Frederick Douglass

FOREWORD BY
DAVID W. BLIGHT

APPLEWOOD BOOKS
CARLISLE, MASSACHUSETTS

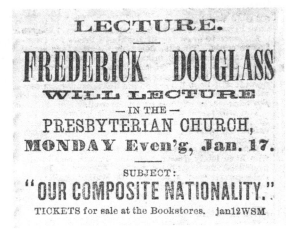

Ad for "Our Composite Nationality" lecture, *Schenectady Evening Star*, 1870. American Antiquarian Society.

Introduction

From his enslaved youth onward, Frederick Douglass had complicated feelings about the United States—he loved America's founding principles but hated the hypocrisy with which they were practiced. After his escape from southern slavery to freedom in 1838, in his extraordinary success as a writer and orator, Douglass regularly delivered embittered attacks on the contradictions of America's institutions. But he always believed that the United States was "full of promise" despite its "errors and defects," and after the Civil War, he decided to take on the task of reconceiving America's mission.

In the late 1860s, in the wake of the ratification of the Fourteenth Amendment and anticipating the ratification of the Fifteenth Amendment, Frederick Douglass toured the country with a speech that laid out his vision of an American future composed of human equality under the law. At that particular moment of Reconstruction, his speech conveyed such a hopeful outlook for a new American polity and society that the former slave could envision a nation based on genuine unity and dignity. Douglass believed the United States had experienced a new founding in the Civil War and was in the midst of crafting a new nation and a new Constitution rooted in the three great amendments spawned by the war's results: abolitionism, equality before the law, and universal manhood suffrage. The country might, he believed, actually become the dream of the authors of emancipation and the Union victory. Born of the massive blood sacrifice of Antietam, Gettysburg, and Andersonville, the nation might make a fundamental shift toward what he called a "composite" nationality based on human brotherhood and the spread of liberty more broadly than any civilization had ever attempted.

Douglass had always believed in the American "mission." The United States was fundamentally a set of ideas, even as it had always been a "tangled network of contradictions." Founded as an experiment and composed of different races of men, the new nation coming into being during early Reconstruction, provided even greater aspiration for humankind and the possibilities of multiethnic pluralism and cultural harmony. Europe and Africa, he wrote, were already integral to the composite that was the United States; immigrants from Ireland had been arriving in great numbers, and "the muscle of the Irishman" had been added to the "arm of the Negro" and helped to build the country. Now Americans needed a new articulation of the American idea, and in his "Composite Nation" speech he argued on behalf of increased Chinese immigration and citizenship. This was an expanded vision not of what we were but of what we ought to be.

The Burlingame Treaty, negotiated between the U.S. and the empire of China in 1868, had accepted the "irrepressible fact" of Chinese immigrants but denied them any right to be naturalized as citizens. Even if the Chinese could enter the United States, they faced violence and prejudice. Douglass urged Americans to accept the Chinese despite what many perceived as the alien character of their language and customs. He assured his countrymen that like all other immigrants they would assimilate and bring talent, skill, and a laboring ethic to the mosaic that was the nation. He reminded Americans that "only one-fifth of the population of the globe is white and the other four-fifths are colored," and in a strikingly modern argument tied to diversity, he argued that all people have "a like humanity" and migratory rights are "human rights." He placed the issue of immigration squarely in the context of America's special character, history, and mission. "A smile or a tear has no nationality," he said at the end of his "Composite Nation" speech.

Frederick Douglass articulated the idea that American pluralism in 1869 was a living fact and still a dream. While we were an on-going experiment, we were "the most fortunate of nations" and "at the beginning of our ascent." The reinvention of the country as a diverse nation living under multiethnic cultural harmony and equality before the law was a hopeful new vision of the body politic and was, he believed, a tangible goal. Forged in the transformations of the Civil War, especially emancipation, what the United States needed was a "new beginning," a more perfect union.

DAVID W. BLIGHT
NOVEMBER 2022

Composite Nation

A S NATIONS ARE AMONG THE LARGEST and the most complete divisions into which society is formed, the grandest aggregations of organized human power; as they raise to observation and distinction the world's greatest men, and call into requisition the highest order of talent and ability for their guidance, preservation and success, they are ever among the most attractive, instructive and useful subjects of thought, to those just entering upon the duties and activities of life.

The simple organization of a people into a National body, composite or otherwise, is of itself and impressive fact. As an original proceeding, it marks the point of departure of a people, from the darkness and chaos of unbridled barbarism, to the wholesome restraints of

Introduction (1)

As nations are among the largest divisions of mankind, and as they are also the grandest aggregations of organized co-operative and concentrated human power, so are they also, among the most attractive of all the subjects of human thought. In whatever quarter of the globe, under whatever system of government, whether rude or refined, of whatever complexion or composition of population, a nation in virtue of being such, invites attention, and commands a certain measure of respect. As with any, so with all. The positions they hold, the Territory under their control, the elements of strength they combine, the ends they propose, the methods they employ, the resources they possess, the results they have accomplished, or have failed public law and society. It implies a willing surrender and subjection of individual aims and ends, often narrow and selfish, to the broader and better ones that arise out of society as a whole. It is both a sign and a result of civilization.

A knowledge of the character, resources and proceedings of other nations, affords us the means of comparison and criticism, without which progress would be feeble, tardy, and perhaps, impossible. It is by comparing one nation with another, and one learning from another, each competing with all, and all competing with each, that hurtful errors are exposed, great social truths discovered, and the wheels of civilization whirled onward.

I am especially to speak to you of the character and mission of the United States, with special reference to the question whether we are the better or the worse for being composed of different races of men. I propose to consider first, what we are, second, what we are likely to be, and, thirdly, what we ought to be.

Without undue vanity or unjust depreciation of others, we may claim to be, in many respects, the most fortunate of nations. We stand in relation to all others, as youth to age. Other nations have had their day of greatness and glory; we are yet to have our day, and that day is coming. The dawn is already upon us. It is bright and full of promise. Other nations have reached their culminating point. We are at the beginning of our ascent. They have apparently exhausted the conditions essential to their further growth and extension, while we are abundant in all the material essential to further national growth and greatness.

The resources of European statesmanship are now sorely taxed to maintain their nationalities at their ancient height of greatness and power.

American statesmanship, worthy of the name, is now taxing its energies to frame measures to meet the demands of constantly increasing expansion of power, responsibility and duty.

Without fault or merit on either side, theirs or ours, the balance is largely in our favor. Like the grand old forests, renewed and enriched from decaying trunks once full of life and beauty, but now moss-covered, oozy and crumbling, we are destined to grow and flourish while they decline and fade.

This is one view of American position and destiny. It is proper to notice that it is not the only view. Different opinions and conflicting judgments meet us here, as elsewhere.

It is thought by many, and said by some, that this Republic has already seen its best days; that the historian may now write the story of its decline and fall.

Two classes of men are just now especially afflicted with such forebodings. The first are those who are croakers by nature—the men who have a taste for funerals, and especially National funerals. They never see the bright side of anything and probably never will. Like the raven in the lines of Edgar A. Poe they have learned two words, and these are "never more." They usually begin by telling us what we never shall see. Their little speeches are about as follows: You will never see such Statesmen in the councils of the nation as Clay, Calhoun and Webster. You will never see the South morally reconstructed and our once happy people again united. You will never see the Government harmonious and successful while in the hands of different races. You will never make the negro work without a master, or make him an intelligent voter, or a good and useful citizen. The last never is generally the parent of all the other little nevers that follow.

During the late contest for the Union, the air was full of nevers, every one of which was contradicted and put to shame by the result, and I doubt not that most of those we now hear in our troubled air, will meet the same fate.

It is probably well for us that some of our gloomy prophets are limited in their powers, to prediction. Could they command the destructive bolt, as readily as they command the destructive world, it is hard to say what might happen to the country. They might fulfill their own gloomy prophesies. Of course it is easy to see why certain other classes on men speak hopelessly concerning us.

A Government founded upon justice, and recognizing the equal rights of all men; claiming higher authority for existence, or sanction for its laws, that nature, reason, and the regularly ascertained will of the people; steadily refusing to put its sword and purse in the service of any religious creed or family is a standing offense to most of the Governments of the world, and to some narrow and bigoted people among ourselves.

To those who doubt and deny the preponderance of good over evil in human nature; who think the few are made to rule, and many to serve; who put rank above brotherhood, and race above humanity; who attach more importance to ancient forms than to the living realities of the present; who worship power in whatever hands it may be lodged and by whatever means it may have been obtained; our Government is a mountain of sin, and, what is worse, its [sic] seems confirmed in its transgressions.

One of the latest and most potent European prophets, one who has felt himself called upon for a special deliverance concerning us and our destiny as a nation, was the late Thomas Carlyle. He described us as rushing to ruin, not only with determined purpose, but with desperate velocity.

How long we have been on this high road to ruin, and when we may expect to reach the terrible end our gloomy prophet, enveloped in the fogs of London, has not been pleased to tell us.

Warnings and advice are not to be despised, from any quarter, and especially not from one so eminent as Mr. Carlyle; and yet Americans will find it hard to heed even men like him, if there be any in the world like him, while the animus is so apparent, bitter and perverse.

A man to whom despotism is Savior and Liberty the destroyer of society,—who, during the last twenty years of his life, in every contest between liberty and oppression, uniformly and promptly took sides with the oppressor; who regarded every extension of the right of suffrage, even to white men in his own country, as shooting Niagara; who gloats over deeds of cruelty, and talked of applying to the backs of men the beneficent whip, to the great delight of many, the slave drivers of America in particular, could have little sympathy with our Emancipated and progressive Republic, or with the triumphs of liberty anywhere.

But the American people can easily stand the utterances of such a man. They however have a right to be impatient and indignant at those among ourselves who turn the most hopeful portents into omens of disaster, and make themselves the ministers of despair when they should be those of hope, and help cheer on the country in the new and grand career of justice upon which it has now so nobly and bravely entered.

Of errors and defects we certainly have not less than our full share, enough to keep the reformer awake, the statesman busy, and the country in a pretty lively state of agitation for some time to come. Perfection is an object to be aimed at by all, but it is not an attribute of any form of Government. Neutrality is the law for all. Something different, something better, or something worse may come, but so far as respects our present system and form of Government, and the altitude we occupy, we need not shrink from comparison with any nation of our times. We are today the best fed, the best clothed, the best sheltered and the best instructed people in the world.

There was a time when even brave men might look fearfully at the destiny of the Republic. When our country was involved in a tangled network of contradictions; when vast and irreconcilable social forces fiercely disputed for ascendancy and control; when a heavy curse rested upon our very soil, defying alike the wisdom and the virtue of the people to remove it; when our professions were loudly mocked by our practice and our name was a reproach and a by word to a mocking earth; when our good ship of state, freighted with the best hopes of the oppressed of all nations, was furiously hurled against the hard and flinty rocks of derision, and every cord, bolt, beam and bend in her body quivered beneath the shock, there was some apology for doubt and despair. But that day has happily passed away. The storm has been weathered, and portents are nearly all in our favor.

There are clouds, wind, smoke and dust and noise, over head and around, and there always will be; but no genuine thunder, with destructive bolt, menaces from any quarter of the sky.

The real trouble with us was never our system or form of Government, or the principles underlying it; but the peculiar composition of our people, the relations existing between them and the compromising spirit which controlled the ruling power of the country.

We have for along time hesitated to adopt and may yet refuse to adopt, and carry out, the only principle which can solve that difficulty and give peace, strength and security to the Republic, and that is the principle of absolute equality.

We are a country of all extremes—, ends and opposites; the most conspicuous example of composite nationality in the world.

Our people defy all the ethnological and logical classifications. In races we range all the way from black to white, with intermediate shades which, as in the apocalyptic vision, no man can name a number.

In regard to creeds and faiths, the condition is no better, and no worse. Differences both as to race and to religion are evidently more likely to increase than to diminish.

We stand between the populous shores of two great oceans. Our land is capable of supporting one fifth of all the globe. Here, labor is abundant and here labor is better remunerated than any where else. All moral, social and geographical causes, conspire to bring to us the peoples of all other over populated countries.

Europe and Africa are already here, and the Indian was here before either. He stands today between the two extremes of black and white, too proud to claim fraternity with either, and yet too weak to withstand the power of either. Heretofore the policy of our government has been governed by race pride, rather than by wisdom.

Until recently, neither the Indian nor the negro has been treated as a part of the body politic. No attempt has been made to inspire either with a sentiment of patriotism, but the hearts of both races have been

Chinese American Newspaper, 1883. Patricia D. Klingenstein Library, New-York Historical Society.

diligently sown with the dangerous seeds of discontent and hatred.

The policy of keeping the Indians to themselves, has kept the tomahawk and scalping knife busy upon our borders, and has cost us largely in blood and treasure.

Our treatment of the negro has slacked humanity, and filled the country with agitation and ill-feeling and brought the nation to the verge of ruin.

Before the relations of these two races are satisfactorily settled, and in spite of all opposition, a new race is making its appearance within our borders, and claiming attention.

It is estimated that not less than one hundred thousand Chinamen, are now within the limits of the United States. Several years ago every vessel, large or small, of steam or sail, bound to our Pacific coast and hailing from the Flowery kingdom, added to the number and strength of this new element of our population.

Men differ widely as to the magnitude of this potential Chinese immigration. The fact that by the late treaty with China, we bind ourselves to receive immigrants from that country only as the subjects of the Emperor, and by the construction, at least, are bound not to [naturalize] them, and the further fact that Chinamen themselves have a superstitious devotion to their country and an aversion to permanent location in any other, contracting even to have their bones carried back, should they die abroad, and from the fact that many have returned to China, and the still more stubborn [fact] that resistance to their coming has increased rather than diminished, it is inferred that we shall never have a large Chinese population in America. This however is not my opinion.

It may be admitted that these reasons, and others, may check and moderate the tide of immigration; but it is absurd to think that they will do more than this. Counting their number now, by the thousands, the time is not remote when they will count them by the millions. The Emperor's hold upon the Chinamen may be strong, but the Chinaman's hold upon himself is stronger.

Treaties against naturalization, like all other treaties, are limited by circumstances. As to the superstitious attachment of the Chinese to China, that, like all other superstitions, will dissolve in the light and heat of truth and experience. The Chinaman may be a bigot, but it does not follow that he will continue to be one, tomorrow. He is a man, and will be very likely to act like a man. He will not be long in finding out that a country which is good enough to live in, is good enough to die in; and that a soil that was good enough to hold his body while alive, will be good enough to hold his bones when he is dead.

Those who doubt a large immigration, should remember that the past furnishes no criterion as a basis of calculation. We live under new and improved conditions of migration, and these conditions are constantly improving.

America is no longer an obscure and inaccessible country. Our ships are in every sea, our commerce in every port, our language is heard all around the globe, steam and lightning have revolutionized the whole domain of human thought. Changed all geographical relations, make a day of the present seem equal to a thousand years of the past, and the continent that Columbus only conjectured four centuries ago is now the centre of the world.

I believe that Chinese immigration on a large scale will yet be our irrepressible fact. The spirit of race pride will not always prevail.

The reasons for this opinion are obvious; China is a vastly overcrowded country. Her people press against each other like cattle in a rail car. Many live upon the water, and have laid out streets upon the waves.

Men, like bees, want elbow room. When the hive is overcrowded, the bees will swarm, and will be likely to take up their abode where they find the best prospect for honey. In matters of this sort, men are very much like bees. Hunger will not be quietly endured, even in the celestial empire, when it is once generally known that there is bread enough and to spare in America. What Satan said of Job is true of the Chinaman, as well as of other men, "All that a man hath will he give for his life." They will come here to live where they know the means of living are in abundance.

The same mighty forces which have swept our shores the overflowing populations of Europe; which have reduced the people of Ireland three millions below its normal standard; will operate in a similar manner upon the hungry population of China and other parts of Asia. Home has its charms, and native land has its charms, but hunger, oppression, and destitution, will dissolve these charms and send men in search of new countries and new homes.

Not only is there a Chinese motive behind this probable immigration, but there is also an American motive which will play its part, one which will be all the more active and energetic because there is in it an element of pride, of bitterness, and revenge.

Southern gentlemen who led in the late rebellion, have not parted with their convictions at this point, any more than at others. They want to be independent of the negro. They believed in slavery and they believe in it still. They believed in an aristocratic class and they believe in it still, and though they have lost slavery, one element essential to such a class, they still have two important conditions to the reconstruction of that class. They have intelligence and they have land. Of these, the land is the more important. They cling to it with all the tenacity of a cherished superstition. They will neither sell to the negro, nor let the carpet baggers have it in peace, but are determined to hold it for themselves and their children forever.

They have not yet learned that when a principle is gone, the incident must go also; that what was wise and proper under slavery, is foolish and mischievous in a state of general liberty; that the old bottles are worthless when the new wine has come; but they have found that land is a doubtful benefit where there are no hands to till it.

Hence these gentlemen have turned their attention to the Celestial Empire. They would rather have laborers who will work for nothing; but as they cannot get the negroes on these terms, they want Chinamen who, they hope, will work for next to nothing.

Companies and associations may be formed to promote this Mongolian invasion. The loss of the negro is to gain them, the Chinese; and if the thing works well, abolition, in their opinion, will have proved itself to be another blessing in disguise. To the statesman it will mean Southern independence. To the pulpit it will be the hand of Providence, and bring about the time of the and what we naturally want will be done.

They will no longer upon the shores of California. They will burrow no longer in her exhausted and deserted gold mines where they gathered wealth from barrenness, taking what others left. They will turn their backs not only upon the golden shores of the Pacific, and the Celestial Empire, but upon the wide waste of waters, whose majestic waves spoke to them of home and country. They will withdraw their eyes from the glowing west and fix them upon the rising sun. Cross the mountains, cross the plains, descend our rivers, penetrate to the heart of the country and fix their homes with us forever.

Assuming then that this immigration already has a foothold and will continue for many years to come, we have a new element in our national composition which is likely to exercise a large influence upon the thought and the action of the whole nation.

The old question as to what shall have to be done with the negro will have to give place to the greater question as to what shall be done with the mongolian, and perhaps we shall see raised one even a still greater, question namely, what will the Mongolian do with both the negro and the whites people as well.

Already has the matter taken this shape in California and on the Pacific coast generally. Already has California assumed a bitterly unfriendly attitude toward the Chinaman. Already has she driven them from her altars of justice. Already has she stamped them as outcasts and handed them over to popular contempt and vulgar jest. Already are they the constant victims of cruel harshness and brutal violence. Already have our Celtic brothers, never slow to execute the behests of popular prejudice against the weak and defenseless, recognized in the heads of these people, fit targets for their shelalahs. Already too, are their associations

12

universal dominion of the Christian religion. To all but the Chinaman and the negro, it will mean wealth, ease and luxury.

But alas, for all the selfish inventions and dreams of men! The Chinaman will not long be willing to wear the cast off shoes of the negro, and if he refuses, there will be trouble again. The negro worked and took his pay in religion and the lash. The Chinaman is a different article and will want the cash. He may, like the negro, accept Christianity, but unlike the negro he will not care to pay for it in labor under the lash. He had the golden rule in substance, five hundred years before the coming of Christ, and has notions of justice that are not to be confused or bewildered by any of our "Cursed be Canaan" religion.

Nevertheless, the experiment will be tried. So far as getting the Chinese into our country is concerned, it will yet be a success. This elephant will be drawn by our Southern brethren, though they will hardly know in the end what to do with him.

Appreciation of the value of Chinamen as laborers will, I apprehend, become general in this country. The North was never indifferent to Southern influence and example, and it will not be so in this instance.

The Chinese in themselves have first rate recommendations. They are industrious, docile, cleanly, frugal;

they are dexterious of hand, patient of toil, marvelously gifted in the power of imitation, and have but few wants. Those who have carefully observed their habits in California, say they can subsist upon what would be almost starvation to others.

The conclusion of the whole will be that they will want to come to us, and as we become more liberal, we shall want them to come, and what we want will normally be done.

They will no longer halt upon the shores of California. They will borrow no longer in her exhausted and deserted gold mines where they have gathered wealth from bareness, taking what others left. They will turn their backs not only upon the Celestial Empire, but upon the golden shores of the Pacific, and the wide waste of waters whose majestic waves spoke to them of home and country. They will withdraw their eyes from the glowing west and fix them upon the rising sun. They will cross the mountains, cross the plains, descend our rivers, penetrate to the heart of the country and fix their homes with us forever.

Assuming then that this immigration already has a foothold and will continue for many years to come, we have a new element in our national composition which is likely to exercise a large influence upon the thought and the action of the whole nation.

The old question as to what shall be done with [the] negro will have to give place to the greater question, "what shall be done with the Mongolian" and perhaps we shall see raised one even still greater question, namely, what will the Mongolian do with both the negro and the whites?

Already has the matter taken this shape in California and on the Pacific Coast generally. Already has California assumed a bitterly unfriendly attitude toward the Chinamen. Already has she driven them from her altars of justice. Already has she stamped them as outcasts and handed them over to popular contempt and vulgar jest. Already are they the constant victims of cruel harshness and brutal violence. Already have our Celtic brothers, never slow to execute the behests of popular prejudice against the weak and defenseless, recognized in the heads of these people, fit targets for their shilalahs. Already, too, are their associations formed in avowed hostility to the Chinese.

In all this there is, of course, nothing strange. Repugnance to the presence and influence of foreigners is an ancient feeling among men. It is peculiar to no particularly race or nation. It is met with not only in the conduct of one nation toward another, but in the conduct of the inhabitants of different parts of the same country, some times of the same city, and even of the same village.

Thomas Nast, "Uncle Sam's Thanksgiving Dinner," Harper's Weekly, 1869. Patricia D. Klingenstein Library, New-York Historical Society.

"Lands intersected by a narrow frith, abhor each other. Mountains interposed, make enemies of nations." To the Hindoo, every man not twice born, is Mleeka. To the Greek, every man not speaking Greek, is a barbarian. To the Jew, every one not circumcised, is a gentile. To the Mahometan, every man not believing in the prophet, is a kaffe.

I need not repeat here the multitude of reproachful epithets expressive of the same sentiment among ourselves. All who are not to the manor born, have been made to feel the lash and sting of these reproachful names.

For this feeling there are many apologies, for there was never yet an error, however flagrant and hurtful, for which some plausible defense could not be framed. Chattel slavery, king craft, priest craft, pious frauds, intolerance, persecution, suicide, assassination, repudiation, and a thousand other errors and crimes, have all had their defenses and apologies.

Prejudice of race and color has been equally upheld. The two best arguments in its defense are, first, the worthlessness of the class against which it was directed; and, second; that he feeling itself is entirely natural.

The way to overcome the first argument is, to work for the elevation of those deemed worthless, and thus make them worthy of regard and they will soon become worthy and not worthless.

As to the natural argument it may be said, that nature has many sides. Many things are in a certain sense natural, which are neither wise nor best. It is natural to walk, but shall men therefore refuse to ride? It is natural to ride on horseback, shall men therefore refuse steam and rail? Civilization is itself a constant war upon some forces in nature; shall we therefore abandon civilization and go back to savage life?

Nature has two voices, the one is high, the other low; one is in sweet accord with reason and justice, and the other apparently at war with both. The more men really know of the essential nature of things, and on of the true relation of mankind, the freer they are from prejudices of every kind. The child is afraid of the giant form of his own shadow. This is natural, but he will part with his fears when he is older and wiser. So ignorance is full of prejudice, but it will disappear with enlightenment. But I pass on.

I have said that the Chinese will come, and have given some reasons why we may expect them in very large numbers in no very distant future. Do you ask, if I favor such immigration, I answer I would. Would you have them naturalized, and have them invested with all the rights of American citizenship? I would. Would you allow them to vote? I would. Would you allow them to hold office? I would.

But are there not reasons against all this? Is there not such a law or principle as that of self-preservation? Does not every race owe something to itself? Should it not attend to the dictates of common sense? Should not a superior race protect itself from contact with inferior ones? Are not the white people the owners of this continent? Have they not the right to say, what kind of people shall be allowed to come here and settle? Is there not such a thing as being more generous than wise? In the effort to promote civilization may we not corrupt and destroy what we have? Is it best to take on board more passengers than the ship will carry?

To all of this and more I have one among many answers, together satisfactory to me, though I cannot promise that it will be so to you.

I submit that this question of Chinese immigration should be settled upon higher principles than those of a cold and selfish expediency.

There are such things in the world as human rights. They rest upon no conventional foundation, but are external, universal, and indestructible.

Among these, is the right of locomotion; the right of migration; the right which belongs to no particular race, but belongs alike to all and to all alike. It is the right you assert by staying here, and your fathers asserted by coming here. It is this great right that I assert for the Chinese and Japanese, and for all other varieties of men equally with yourselves, now and forever. I know of no rights of race superior to the rights of humanity, and when there is a supposed conflict between human and national rights, it is safe to go to the side of humanity. I have great respect for the blue eyed and light haired races of America. They are a mighty people. In any struggle for the good things of this world they need have no fear. They have no need to doubt that they will get their full share.

But I reject the arrogant and scornful theory by which they would limit migratory rights, or any other essential human rights to themselves, and which would make them the owners of this great continent to the exclusion of all other races of men.

I want a home here not only for the negro, the mulatto and the Latin races; but I want the Asiatic to find a home here in the United States, and feel at home here, both for his sake and for ours. Right wrongs no man. If respect is had to majorities, the fact that only one fifth of the population of the globe is white, the other four fifths are colored, ought to have some weight and influence in disposing of this and similar questions. It would be a sad reflection upon the laws of nature and upon the idea of justice, to say nothing of a common Creator, if four fifths of mankind were deprived of the rights of migration to make room for the one fifth. If the white race may exclude all other races from this continent, it may rightfully do the same in respect to all other lands, islands, capes and continents, and thus have all the world to itself. Thus what would seem to belong to the whole, would become the property only of a part. So much for what is right, now let us see what is wise.

And here I hold that a liberal and brotherly welcome to all who are likely to come to the United states, is the only wise policy which this nation can adopt.

It has been thoughtfully observed, that every nation, owing to its peculiar character and composition, has a definite mission in the world. What that mission is, and what policy is best adapted to assist in its fulfillment, is the business of its people and its statesmen to know, and knowing, to make a noble use of said knowledge.

I need to stop here to name or describe the missions of other and more ancient nationalities. Ours seems plain and unmistakable. Our geographical position, our relation to the outside world, our fundamental principles of Government, world embracing in their scope and character, our vast resources, requiring all manner of labor to develop them, and our already existing composite population, all conspire to one grand end, and that is to make us the make perfect national illustration of the unit and dignity of the human family, that the world has ever seen.

In whatever else other nations may have been great and grand, our greatness and grandeur will be found in the faithful application of the principle of perfect civil equality to the people of all races and of all creeds, and to men of no creeds. We are not only bound to this position by our organic structure and by our revolutionary antecedents, but by the genius of our people. Gathered here, from all quarters of the globe by a common aspiration for rational liberty as against caste, divine right Governments and privileged classes, it would be unwise to be found fighting against ourselves and among ourselves; it would be madness to set up any one race above another, or one religion above another, or proscribe any on account of race color or creed.

The apprehension that we shall be swamped or swallowed up by Mongolian civilization; that the Caucasian race may not be able to hold their own against that vast incoming population, does not seem entitled to much respect. Though they come as the waves come, we shall be stronger if we receive them as friends and give them a reason for loving our country and our institutions. They will find here a deeply rooted, indigenous, growing civilization, augmented by an ever increasing stream of immigration from Europe; and possession is nine points of the law in this case, as well as in others. They will come as strangers, we are at home. They will come to us, not we to them. They will come in their weakness, we shall meet them in our strength. They will come as individuals, we will meet them in multitudes, and with all the advantages of organization. Chinese children are in American schools in San Francisco, none of our children are in Chinese schools, and probably never will be, though in some things they might well teach us valuable lessons. Contact with these yellow children of The Celestial Empire would convince us that the points of human difference, great as they, upon first sight, seem, are as nothing compared with the points of human agr eement. Such contact would remove mountains of prejudice.

It is said that it is not good for man to be alone. This is true not only in the sense in which our woman's rights friends so zealously and wisely teach, but it is true as to nations.

The voice of civilization speaks an unmistakable language against the isolation of families, nations and races, and pleads for composite nationality as essential to her triumphs.

Those races of men which have maintained the most separate and distinct existence for the longest periods of time; which have had the least intercourse with other races of men, are a standing confirmation of the folly of isolation. The very soil of the national mind becomes, in such cases, barren, and can only be resuscitated by assistance from without.

Look at England, whose mighty power is now felt, and for centuries has been felt, all around the world. It is worthy of special remark, that precisely those parts of that proud Island which have received the largest and most diverse populations, are today, the parts most distinguished for industry, enterprise, invention and general enlightenment. In Wales, and in the Highlands of Scotland, the boast is made of their pure blood and that they were never conquered, but no man can contemplate them without wishing they had been conquered.

They are far in the rear of every other part of the English realm in all the comforts and conveniences of life, as well as in mental and physical development. Neither law nor learning descends to us from the mountains of Wales or from the Highlands of Scotland. The ancient Briton whom Julius Caesar would not have a slave, is not to be compared with the round, burly, a[m]plitudinous Englishman in many of the qualities of desirable manhood.

The theory that each race of men has come special faculty, some peculiar gift or quality of mind or heart, needed to the perfection and happiness of the whole is a broad and beneficent theory, and besides its beneficence, has in its support, the voice of experience.

Nobody doubts this theory when applied to animals and plants, and no one can show that it is not equally true when applied to races.

All great qualities are never found in any one man or in any one race. The whole of humanity, like the whole of everything else, is ever greater than a part. Men only know themselves by knowing others, and contact is essential to this knowledge. In one race we perceive the predominance of imagination; in another, like Chinese, we remark its total absence. In one people, we have the reasoning faculty, in another, for music; in another, exists courage; in another, great physical vigor; and so on through the whole list of human qualities. All are needed to temper, modify, round and complete the whole man and the whole nation.

Not the least among the arguments whose consideration should dispose to welcome among us the peoples of all countries, nationalities and color, is the fact that all races and varieties of men are improvable. This is the grand distinguishing attribute of humanity and separates man from all other animals. If it could be shown that any particular race of men are literally incapable of improvement, we might hesitate to welcome them here. But no such men are anywhere to be found, and if there were, it is not likely that they would ever trouble us with their presence.

The fact that the Chinese and other nations desire to come and do come, is a proof of their capacity for improvement and of their fitness to come.

We should take council of both nature and art in the consideration of this question. When the architect intends a grand structure, he makes the foundation broad and strong. We should imitate this prudence in laying the foundation of the future Republic. There is a law of harmony in departments of nature. The oak is in the acorn. The career and destiny of individual men are enfolded in the elements of which they are composed. The same is true of a nation. It will be something or it will be nothing. It will be great, or it will be small, according to its own essential qualities. As these are rich and varied, or poor and simple, slender and feeble, broad and strong, so will be the life and destiny of the nation itself.

The stream cannot rise higher than its source. The ship cannot sail faster than the wind. The flight of the arrow depends upon the strength and elasticity of the bow; and as with these, so with a nation.

If we would reach a degree of civilization higher and grander than any yet attained, we should welcome to our ample continent all nations, kindreds [sic] tongues and peoples; and as fast as they learn our language and comprehend the duties of citizenship, we should incorporate them into the American body politic. The outspread wings of the American eagle are broad enough to shelter all who are likely to come.

As a matter of selfish policy, leaving right and humanity out of the question, we cannot wisely pursue any other course. Other Governments mainly depend for security upon the sword; our depends mainly upon the friendship of its people. In all matters,—in time of peace, in time of war, and at all times,—it makes its appeal to all the people, and to all classes of the people. Its strength lies in their friendship and cheerful support in every time of need, and that policy is a mad one which would reduce the number of its friends by excluding those who would come, or by alienating those who are already here.

Our Republic is itself a strong argument in favor of composite nationality. It is no disparagement to Americans of English descent, to affirm that much of the wealth, leisure, culture, refinement and civilization of the country are due to the arm of the negro and the muscle of the Irishman. Without these and the wealth created by their sturdy toil, English civilization had still lingered this side of the Alleghanies [sic], and the wolf still be howling on their summits.

To no class of our population are we more indebted to valuable qualities of head, heart and hand than the German. Say what we will of their lager, their smoke and their metaphysics they have brought to us a fresh, vigorous and child-like nature; a boundless facility in the acquisition of knowledge; a subtle and far reaching intellect, and a fearless love of truth. Though remarkable for patient and laborious thought the true German is a joyous child of freedom, fond of manly sports, a lover of music, and a happy man generally. Though he never forgets that he is a German, he never fails to remember that he is an American.

A Frenchman comes here to make money, and that is about all that need be said of him. He is only a Frenchman. He neither learns our language nor loves our country. His hand is on our pocket and his eye on Paris. He gets what he wants and like a sensible Frenchman, returns to France to spend it.

Now let me answer briefly some objections to the general scope of my arguments. I am told that science is against me; that races are not all of one origin, and that the unity theory of human origin has been exploded. I admit that this is a question that has two sides. It is impossible to trace the threads of human history sufficiently near their starting point to know much about the origin of races.

In disposing of this question whether we shall welcome or repel immigration from China, Japan, or elsewhere, we may leave the differences among the theological doctors to be settled by themselves.

Currier & Ives, *The Express Train*, 1870. Library of Congress.

Whether man originated at one time and one or another place; whether there was one Adam or five, or five hundred, does not affect the question.

The grand right of migration and the great wisdom of incorporating foreign elements into our body politic, are founded not upon any genealogical or archeological theory, however learned, but upon the broad fact of a common human nature.

Man is man, the world over. This fact is affirmed and admitted in any effort to deny it.

The sentiments we exhibit, whether love or hate, confidence or fear, respect or contempt, will always imply a like humanity.

A smile or a tear has not nationality; joy and sorrow speak alike to all nations, and they, above all the confusion of tongues, proclaim the brotherhood of man.

It is objected to the Chinaman that he is secretive and treacherous, and will not tell the truth when he thinks it for his interest to tell a lie.

There may be truth in all this; it sounds very much like the account of man's heart given in the creeds. If he will not tell the truth except when it is for his interest to do so, let us make it for this interest to tell the truth We can do it by applying to him the same principle of justice that we apply ourselves.

But I doubt if the Chinese are more untruthful than other people. At this point I have one certain test,— mankind are not held together by lies. Trust is the foundation of society. Where there is no truth, there can be no trust, and where there is no trust there can be no society. Where there is society, there is trust, and where there is trust, there is something upon which it is supported. Now a people who have confided in each other for five thousand years; who have extended their empire in all direction till it embraces on e fifth of the population of the glove; who hold important commercial relations with all nations; who are now entering into treaty stipulations with ourselves, and with all the great European powers, cannot be a nation of cheats and liars, but must have some respect for veracity. The very existence of China for so long a period, and her progress in civilization, are proofs of her truthfulness. But it is said that the Chinese is a heathen, and that he will introduce his heathen rights and superstitions here. This is the last objection which should come from those who profess the all conquering power of the Christian religion. If that religion cannot stand contact with the Chinese, religion or no religion, so much the worse for those who have adopted it. It is the Chinaman, not the Christian, who should be alarmed for his faith. He exposes that faith to great dangers by exposing it to the freer air of America. But shall we send missionaries to the heathen and yet deny the heathen the right to come to us? I think that a few honest believers in the teachings of Confucius would be well employed in expounding his doctrines among us.

The next objection to the Chinese is that he cannot be induced to swear by the Bible. This is to me one of his best recommendations. The American people will swear by anything in the heavens above or in the earth beneath. We are a nation of swearers. We swear by a book whose most authoritative command is to swear not at all.

It is not of so much importance what a man swears by, as what he swears to, and if the Chinaman is so true to his convictions that he cannot be tempted or even coerced into so popular a custom as swearing by the Bible, he gives good evidence of his integrity and his veracity.

Let the Chinaman come; he will help to augment the national wealth. He will help to develop our boundless resources; he will help to pay off our national debt. He will help to lighten the burden of national taxation. He will give us the benefit of his skill as a manufacturer and tiller of the soil, in which he is unsurpassed.

Even the matter of religious liberty, which has cost the world more tears, more blood and more agony, than any other interest, will be helped by his presence. I know of no church, however tolerant; of no priesthood, however enlightened, which could be safely trusted with the tremendous power which universal conformity would confer. We should welcome all men of every shade of religious opinion, as among the best means of checking the arrogance and intolerance which are the almost inevitable concomitants of general conformity. Religious liberty always flourishes best amid the clash and competition of rival religious creeds.

To the minds of superficial men, the fusion of different races has already brought disaster and ruin upon the country. The poor negro has been charged with all our woes. In the haste of these men they forgot that our trouble was not ethnographical, but moral; that it was not a difference of complexion, but a difference of conviction. It was not the Ethiopian as a man, but the Ethiopian as a slave and a covetted [sic] article of merchandise, that gave us trouble.

I close these remarks as I began. If our action shall be in accordance with the principles of justice, liberty, and perfect human equality, no eloquence can adequately portray the greatness and grandeur of the future of the Republic.

We shall spread the network of our science and civilization over all who seek their shelter whether from Asia, Africa, or the Isles of the sea. We shall mold them all, each after his kind, into Americans; Indian and Celt; negro and Saxon; Latin and Teuton; Mongolian and Caucasian; Jew and Gentile; all shall here bow to the same law, speak the same language, support the same Government, enjoy the same liberty, vibrate with the same national enthusiasm, and seek the same national ends.

FINIS.